books by BOXER

www.booksbyboxer.com

Published by
Books By Boxer, Leeds, LS13 4BS UK
Books by Boxer (EU), Dublin D02 P593 IRELAND
© Books By Boxer 2022
All Rights Reserved
MADE IN CHINA
ISBN: 9781915410009

ARE YOU A PSYCHOPATH?

ARE YOU A STABBER OR A SPREADER?

IF YOU'RE THE KIND OF PERSON WHO SKIMS THE TOP OF YOUR BUTTER, THEN CONGRATULATIONS, YOU'LL MAKE IT TO HEAVEN! BUT IF YOU HAVE THE NEED TO STAB INTO YOUR BUTTER, CARVING CHUNKS JUST TO SATISFY YOUR BUTTERY NEEDS, THEN YOU DESERVE TO BE LOCKED UP - YOU PSYCHO!

AN EVEN WORSE CRIME TO HUMANITY IS PURPOSELY USING THE SAME KNIFE YOU SCRAPED ACROSS THE SURFACE OF YOUR TOAST, LEAVING ALL THE BREADY BITS SWIMMING IN YOUR BUTTER!

KETCH-UP TO NO GOOD?

DO YOU KEEP YOUR KETCHUP IN THE FRIDGE? IF SO,
YOU ARE DEFINITELY ALL 57 VARIETIES OF PSYCHO!
NOBODY WANTS COLD, LUMPY SAUCE PLOPPED OVER
THEIR CHIPS, GET IT IN THE CUPBOARD BEFORE YOU
HURT SOMEBODY! (OR WORSE, GET ARRESTED FOR THIS
ATROCIOUS CRIME...)

OVER OR UNDER?

WHO ARE WE TO JUDGE HOW YOU GO TO THE TOILET? YOU COULD SIT UPSIDE DOWN IF YOU REALLY WANTED TO. BUT THERE'S ONE SMALL DECISION THAT COULD TURN YOU FROM A NORMAL HUMAN INTO A FULL BLOWN PSYCHO... THE WAY YOU HANG YOUR BOG ROLL! YES, THERE IS A CORRECT WAY TO HANG IT, AND NO, WE ARE NOT RESPONSIBLE FOR ANY HEADS FLUSHED DOWN THE LOO IF YOU PUT IT THE WRONG WAY ROUND.

DID YOU KNOW THAT THE 1891 PATENT FOR TOILET ROLL SPECIFICALLY STATES THAT IT SHOULD BE HUNG OVER, NOT UNDER? WRITTEN PROOF THAT YOU VERY WELL COULD BE USING THOSE LITTLE POOP SQUARES WRONG.

TRICK OR TREAT?

YOU SPOT A PURPLE ONE AT THE BOTTOM OF THE SWEET TUB, GO TO REACH FOR IT, AND THEN POP! YOUR MOOD DEFLATES AS YOU REALISE IT WAS JUST ANOTHER CHOCOLATY CATFISH. THIS IS A SURE SIGN THAT SOMEBODY HAS PSYCHOTIC TENDENCIES.

WHO ELSE WOULD PURPOSELY RUIN A PERSON'S DAY BY MIXING EMPTY WRAPPERS WITH YUMMY SWEETIES?

ARE YOU PEELING OKAY?

YOU BITE AN APPLE. YOU PEEL A BANANA. BUT YOU
DO NOT, AND I REPEAT, DO NOT BITE INTO A WHOLE
CHOCOLATE ORANGE. WHAT KIND OF MONSTER ARE YOU?
DEFILING THAT INNOCENT CHOCOLATY TREAT, MAKING
IT SO NOBODY WILL DARE ASK YOU FOR A PIECE...
DESPICABLE!

WHAT'S WORSE ARE PEOPLE WHO EAT TO THE VERY END
OF THIS FAKE ORANGE, ONLY TO THROW THE CORE
PIECE AWAY - AS THOUGH IT ISN'T MADE UP OF
YUMMY GOODNESS.

A-PEE-L YOUR INNOCENCE!

THIS ONE'S AIMED AT THE DEMENTED MEN IN OUR
LIVES. YES, YOU! DO YOU 'FORGET' TO PUT THE
TOILET SEAT DOWN? MAYBE YOU'RE NOT FIT TO GO OUT
IN PUBLIC – IMAGINE: YOU MIGHT 'FORGET' HOW TO
CROSS THE ROAD, OR EVEN 'FORGET' HOW TO PUT ONE
FOOT IN FRONT OF THE OTHER! YOU'RE A DANGER TO
SOCIETY AND YOU KNOW IT!

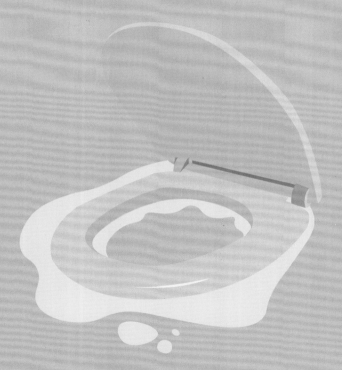

NOW, DO YOU THINK YOU CAN HIDE BEING A PSYCHO
BY LEAVING THE SEAT DOWN? THAT'S EVEN WORSE!
PEE DRIBBLED ALL OVER THE SEAT, SPLASHBACK
UNDERNEATH IT, DISGUSTING!

CUCKOO CUPBOARDS

YOU FIND YOURSELF SPEED-WALKING INTO YOUR KITCHEN THEN... BANG! YOU GET A CUPBOARD DOOR RIGHT INTO YOUR FACE. WAS IT A PRANK? SOME SICK JOKE? AN ACCIDENT MAYBE? NO. A PSYCHOPATH DELIBERATELY LEFT IT OPEN. ARE YOU THAT PSYCHO?

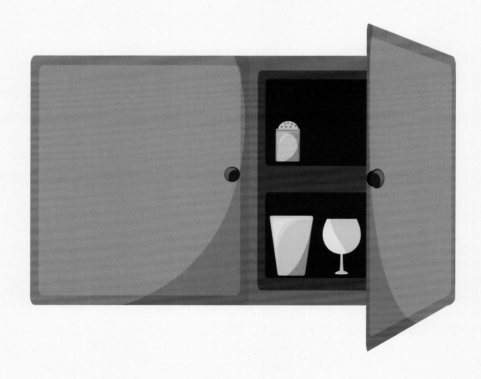

A LID-DLE BIT PSYCHO

YOU PICK UP YOUR JAR OF PICKLED ONIONS OR
YOUR BOTTLE OF FIZZY POP AND SPLASH! THE ROOM
EITHER SMELLS LIKE OLD VINEGAR AND ONIONS, OR
EVERYTHING IT TOUCHED NOW FEELS LIKE A PUB FLOOR
ON SATURDAY NIGHT... EITHER WAY THERE'S ONLY ONE
PERSON TO BLAME, AND THAT'S WHOEVER THINKS IT'S
ACCEPTABLE TO LEAVE LIDS UNSCREWED.

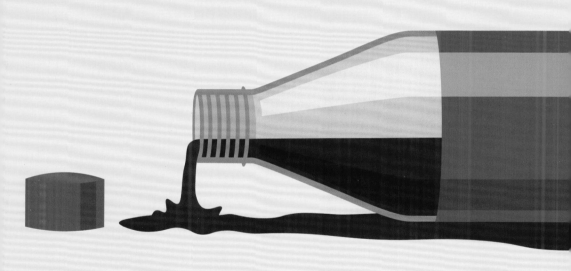

THEY GIVE US A FALSE SENSE OF SECURITY WHILE
IN REALITY, THEY KNOW WHAT CHAOS IS ABOUT TO
OCCUR. SHAMEFUL.

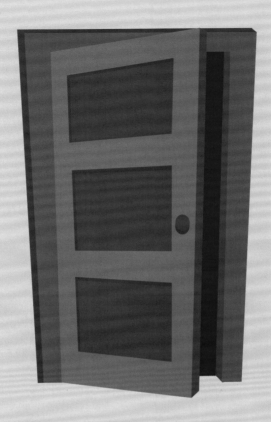

SHUT IT!

THERE'S TWO KINDS OF PEOPLE. THOSE WHO SHUT
EVERY DOOR THEY WALK THROUGH, AND THOSE WHO
INSIST ON LEAVING DOORS OPEN ALL THE TIME! ON
THE TOILET - OPEN. ZERO DEGREES CENTIGRADE? -
OPEN. IT'S SURPRISING YOUR FAMILY HASN'T LOCKED
YOU OUT FOR GOOD.

HOLD IT!

WHILE WE'RE ON THE DOOR SUBJECT, WHO ON EARTH
DECIDES TO HOLD THE DOOR FOR YOU WHEN YOU'RE
MILES AWAY? THAT AWKWARD SPRINT TO THE DOOR, THE
VERY FLAT SMILE AND AWKWARD SQUEEZE THROUGH THE
DOORFRAME... DON'T THEY KNOW YOU'RE CAPABLE OF
OPENING IT YOURSELF?

CRAZED AND CHARGED

IT'S A NORMAL, EVERYDAY TASK TO POP YOUR PHONE ONTO CHARGE, BUT THAT PERCENTAGE ICON AT THE TOP OF A SCREEN CAN REALLY SHOW A PERSON'S TRUE COLOURS. FOR INSTANCE, WHAT KIND OF LOON FINDS IT NECESSARY TO TAKE IT BACK OFF CHARGE WHEN IT'S ONE PERCENT BEFORE FULL? 99% GLOWING VIOLENTLY ON THE SCREEN, WARNING EVERYBODY TO CALL THE MEN IN WHITE COATS...

EVER PLAYED PERCENTAGE ROULETTE? GAMBLING ON HOW LONG YOU CAN GO WITHOUT CHARGING YOUR PHONE? AT 10%, MOST PEOPLE WILL GIVE IN AND PLUG IT IN TO CHARGE... IF YOU WAIT TILL 1%, THEN YOU'RE A NUTCASE AND NEED TO FIND THE CLOSEST PADDED ROOM AVAILABLE.

TAKE A BREAK

ARE YOU THE KIND OF PERSON WHO INSISTS ON BITING
ALL BARS OF A KITKAT AT ONCE? THEY'RE CALLED
FINGERS FOR A REASON YOU LUNATIC! DOES IT GIVE
YOU SOME STRANGE SENSE OF VICTORY?
ABSOLUTE NUTCASE!

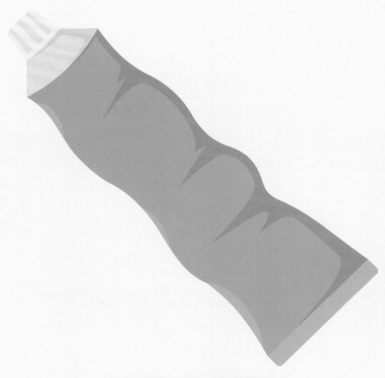

PASTE YOURSELF

DO YOU GENTLY SQUEEZE TOOTHPASTE FROM THE END OF THE TUBE, EVENLY DISTRIBUTING THE PASTE ACROSS YOUR BRUSH AND KEEPING THE TUBE NICE AND PRESENTABLE? GOOD FOR YOU, FRIEND! YOU'RE A GREAT MEMBER OF SOCIETY. HOWEVER, IF YOU FEEL THE NEED TO TAKE YOUR ANGER OUT ON THAT POOR MINTY TUBE, SQUEEZING IT FROM THE MIDDLE, LEAVING TOOTHPASTE EVERYWHERE, THEN YOU'RE A DANGER TO YOURSELF AND OTHERS AND NEED TO BE RESTRAINED.

A BRUSH WITH INSANITY

WHAT'S EVEN WORSE ARE THE COMPLETE NUTTERS WHO TALK WHILE BRUSHING THEIR GNASHERS – FROTHY POOLS OF MINTY SPIT DRIBBLING DOWN THEIR CHINS AND SLURRED WORDS STOPPED ONLY BY THE CLANGING OF PLASTIC ON TEETH. THEY KAW ORDERS AT YOU LIKE "KAH HUE PASH DA MAWF WAWSH?!", AND "DEHS A SHPIDA EN DAH SHINK!"

FEELING CHEESED OFF?

IF YOU SEE A BLOCK OF CHEESE AND THINK YOU CAN
TEAR IT TO SHREDS, THEN I HATE TO BREAK IT TO
YOU... BUT YOU'RE A NUTTER.

CUTTING THE CHEESE WONKY IS A MASSIVE RED FLAG.
WHAT DID THE CHEESE DO TO YOU TO BE VIOLATED TO
SUCH A DEGREE? WHAT'S PREVENTING YOU FROM CUTTING
SIMPLE, ORGANISED SLICES? ABSOLUTELY NOTHING.

STOP BEING A MAVERICK AND GET A CHOPPING BOARD
FOR GOD'S SAKE. NEXT YOU'LL BE BITING INTO THE
CHEESE WHEEL LIKE IT'S A SLICE OF BREAD!

TOWEL OR TAKE OFF?

WHEN MAKING A DRINK, MISTAKES HAPPEN. SOMETIMES SOME LIQUID CAN SPILL ONTO THE FLOOR - WE ARE ALL ONLY HUMAN! HOWEVER, ARE YOU THE KIND OF PERSON TO WIPE IT UP, OR DO YOU BELIEVE IT TO BE THE FLOOR'S PROBLEM? GRAB A TEA TOWEL OR SOME KITCHEN ROLL IF YOU DON'T WANT TO GET BAD KARMA.

P.S. WIPING IT WITH YOUR SOCK DOESN'T COUNT, YOU UNHINGED LUNATIC.

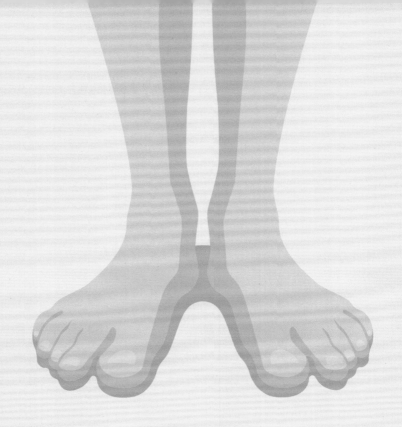

LAID TO BARE

NO - YOU'RE NOT 'MORE CONNECTED TO THE WORLD AROUND YOU', YOU'RE JUST WEIRD. IF YOU HAVE A PERFECTLY GOOD PAIR OF SHOES, AND STILL CHOOSE TO LEAVE THE HOUSE WEARING NOTHING ON YOUR FEET FOR ANY PERIOD OF TIME, YOU FEAR NOTHING, AND NOT IN A GOOD WAY. WHO KNOWS WHAT'S BEEN ON THE FLOOR? PLEASE, EVEN IF YOU'RE JUST TAKING THE BINS OUT... FLIP FLOPS ARE A GREAT SOLUTION.

IT'S LIT!

AS OF LATE, EVERYONE HAS BECOME MORE
ENVIRONMENTALLY FRIENDLY. HELL, THE EARTH MAY BE
GONE IN THE NEXT 6 MONTHS IF PEOPLE DON'T CHANGE
THEIR HABITS! HOWEVER, IF YOU LIKE LEAVING
LIGHTS ON, ESPECIALLY DURING THE DAYTIME, DON'T
BE SURPRISED WHEN YOU GET BLAMED FOR THE MELTING
ICE CAPS. THE FATE OF THIS WORLD RESTS ON YOUR
SHOULDERS… SO CHANGE YOUR WAYS - UNLESS YOU WANT
GRETA THUNBERG ON YOUR HEELS!

HUM HALLELUJAH

IT'S UNREASONABLE TO EXPECT THAT YOU'LL KNOW *ALL*
LYRICS TO *ALL* SONGS AT *ALL* TIMES – YOU'RE ONLY
HUMAN! BUT IF YOU INSIST ON POLLUTING THE AIR
WITH YOUR TERRIBLE SINGING, THE LEAST YOU CAN DO
IS GET THE LYRICS RIGHT. IF YOU CONSTANTLY SING
THE SAME 10 SECONDS OF THE SONG OVER AND OVER,
BECAUSE YOU DON'T KNOW THE REST, THEN JUST DON'T
SING AT ALL.

THE WORLD WOULD BE A BETTER PLACE IF YOU KEPT IT TO
YOURSELF... SOME THINGS SOUND BETTER IN YOUR HEAD!

Not Everyone's Type

WE LIVE IN THE 21ST CENTURY NOW... AS A SOCIETY WE HAVE MOVED PAST THE NEED TO USE COMIC SANS ON A DAY-TO-DAY BASIS. IF YOU'RE UNDER THE AGE OF 10, IT SEEMS LIKE A FUN AND QUIRKY OPTION. BUT AT YOUR BIG AGE? THIS IS A FIRST-CLASS TICKET TO THE LOONY BIN. EVEN Helvetica BEATS COMIC SANS. IF YOU STILL USE THIS CURLY ROUNDED FONT... I HOPE YOU'RE HAPPY WITH YOURSELF.

CUTTING THE ATMOSPHERE

PICTURE THIS: YOU'RE AT A NICE RESTAURANT...
DRINKS ARE FLOWING... GREAT ATMOSPHERE... AND
THEN THE FOOD ARRIVES. THE SOUND OF THE
CUTLERY SCRAPING THROUGH THE TABLEWARE SENDS
SHIVERS DOWN YOUR SPINE. DO YOU KNOW THE
FEELING? IF YOU'RE A CONSIDERATE CUTTER, THEN
CONGRATULATIONS! YOU'RE ALLOWED OUT OF THE HOUSE.

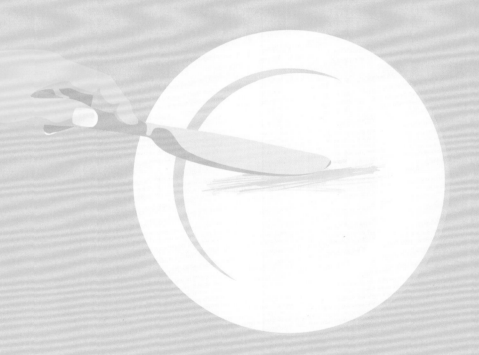

IF THIS SCENARIO ISN'T RINGING BELLS, MAYBE
YOU'RE THE PROBLEM. PLEASE... DON'T SCRAPE YOUR
CUTLERY ACROSS YOUR PLATE, NO ONE WANTS TO
LISTEN TO THAT.

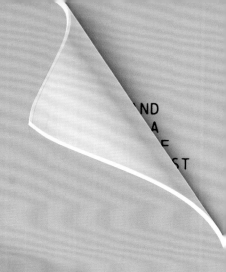

FOLDED FRUITCAKE

FOLDING PAGES IN A BOOK IS ONE OF THOSE
SEEMINGLY MUNDANE THINGS THAT FEELS LIKE AN ACT
OF VIOLENCE. EVEN THE DAINTIEST OF FOLDS WILL
BE IMPOSSIBLE TO REMOVE – SO WHY DO IT IN THE
FIRST PLACE? IF YOU ARE SO HEAVILY INVESTED IN
THE BOOK THAT YOU DON'T WANT TO LOSE YOUR PLACE,
TREAT IT WITH SOME RESPECT AND USE A BOOKMARK.
THIS BECOMES EVEN MORE UNSPEAKABLE IF THE BOOK
ISN'T EVEN YOURS...

BIGGER IS NOT ALWAYS BETTER

AT THIS POINT, WE HAVE SURPASSED THE NEED FOR
THE BIG LIGHT. IT HANGS FROM THE CEILING, BUT
REALISTICALLY, WHO ACTUALLY SITS DOWN TO RELAX
UNDER THE BLINDING GLARE OF A CEILING LIGHT?
UNLESS YOU'RE A PSYCHO, THAT IS. LAMPS, CANDLES
AND FAIRY LIGHTS ALL HELP TO BRING SOME FENG
SHUI INTO YOUR RELAXATION SPACE, SO TURNING THE
BIG LIGHT ON IS VERY QUESTIONABLE.

EVEN MORE NEGATIVE POINTS IF YOU HAVE WHITE
LIGHT BULBS... EVERYONE KNOWS YELLOW IS BETTER.

PUT A SOCK IN IT

SOMETIMES SOCKS DO MAKE YOUR FEET HOT, AND ESPECIALLY IN WARM WEATHER, FEET CAN GET A LITTLE MOIST. HOWEVER, IF YOU'RE THE TYPE OF PERSON WHO THINKS THAT THE BETTER OPTION IS JUST PUTTING YOUR FEET IN TRAINERS... RAW... YOU HAVE SOME EXPLAINING TO DO. NOT ONLY WILL THIS MAKE YOUR SHOES SWEATY AND SWAMPY, SURELY IT JUST FEELS REALLY WEIRD?

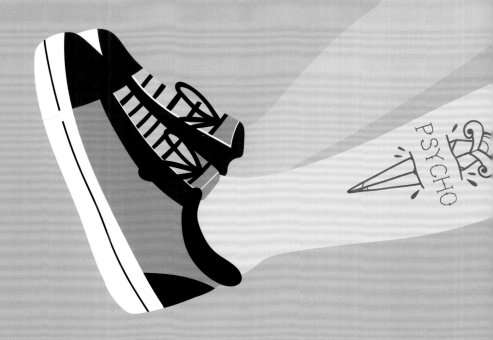

MODERN SOCK TECHNOLOGY MEANS THAT ALMOST EVERY SHOE CAN BE PAIRED WITH SOME SORT OF SOCK, SO THERE REALLY ISN'T ANY EXCUSE... PUT YOUR HOOVES AWAY!

YOU SEXY THANG

THERE ARE THOUSANDS OF DESCRIPTORS IN THE
ENGLISH LANGUAGE THAT CAN BE USED TO DESCRIBE
INANIMATE OBJECTS - BEAUTIFUL, STYLISH, FANCY...
THE LIST GOES ON! BUT IF YOU LIKE TO DESCRIBE
OBJECTS AS "SEXY", THEN I'M SORRY, BUT YOU NEED
TO REVALUATE YOUR APPROACH TO LIFE. THAT CAR
ISN'T "SEXY"... IT'S A CAR - GROW UP.

ARE YOU A DOUBLE DIPPER?

POOR SUGAR. ALL IT WANTS IS TO EXIST IN PEACE,
AWAY FROM MANIACS WITH SOGGY SPOONS... BUT ALONG
COMES A NUTCASE, DIPPING THEIR WET CUTLERY INTO
A NICE FRESH POT OF SUGAR, MAKING IT GO LUMPY
AND CRISPY. IF YOU'RE THAT KIND OF PERSON, YOU
SHOULD BE ASHAMED OF YOURSELF, BANNED FROM SUGAR
AND DESTINED TO ONLY USE SWEETENER TABLETS.

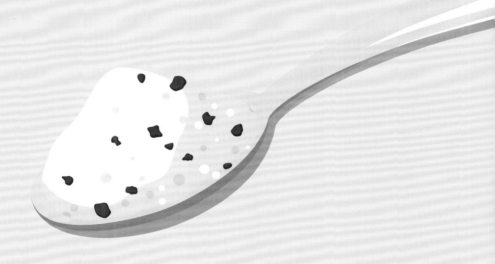

IF SOGGY SPOONS DON'T CAUSE ENOUGH UPSET IN THE
WORLD THEN REST ASSURED, THERE WILL BE ONE LUNATIC
OUT THERE, RUNNING AROUND WITH A WET SPOON WHO
ISN'T SATISFIED UNTIL THE SUGAR POT HAS TRACES OF
DAMP COFFEE AND WATER CLUMPS. SICKENING.

YOU'RE HOT...

IT'S BEGINNING TO LOOK A LOT LIKE WINTER. THE CRUNCHING OF ICE, SNOWFLAKES FALLING FROM THE SKY, AND, WAIT-WHAT'S THAT IN THE DISTANCE? SOMEBODY IN SHORTS? IN THIS WEATHER!? THEY MUST BE BARKING MAD! I DON'T THINK WE HAVE TO TELL YOU THAT IF YOU'RE THAT PERSON, THEN YOU'RE AN UNHINGED HUMAN AND DON'T DESERVE NICE THINGS LIKE WARMTH!

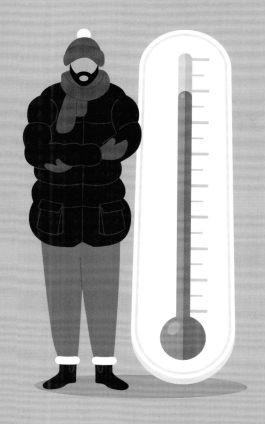

...AND YOU'RE COLD!

ALTERNATIVELY, IF YOU FIND YOURSELF LOOKING LIKE AN ESKIMO IN SUMMER, THEN YOU NEED TO GET YOUR CRANIUM CHECKED. HOW HAVE YOU NOT TURNED INTO A PUDDLE OF SWEAT BY NOW? WOOLLY HATS, SCARVES AND FUR HOODS... YOU REALLY NEED TO STRIP DOWN A FEW LAYERS. JEEZ!

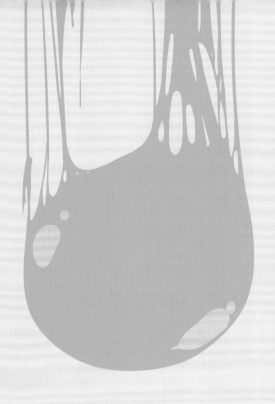

CHOMP ON IT

CHOMPING ON BUBBLE-GUM IS GROSS BUT TOLERABLE…
THAT IS, UNTIL YOU START BLOWING UP YOUR GUM
LIKE A CHILD'S 2ND BIRTHDAY BALLOON! IS THIS A
GAME OF HOW BIG YOU CAN MAKE THE GUM STRETCH, OR
IS IT SOMETHING YOU SHOULD BE TALKING TO YOUR
PSYCHIATRIST ABOUT? EITHER WAY, NOBODY WANTS TO
SEE YOUR SPIT COVERED WHALE FAT!

MILKY MAYHEM

YOUR SHOPPING LIST IS WRITTEN. YOU HEAD TO THE SHOP FOR YOUR GROCERIES. COME BACK DYING FOR A BREW, AND FIND THAT IT WAS ALL A LIE. YOU DID ACTUALLY NEED MILK, BUT SOME MANIAC PUT THE EMPTY CARTON INTO THE FRIDGE. WHY ARE THESE PEOPLE FREE TO ROAM THE STREETS? THEY DO NOTHING BUT BRING MILKLESS MAYHEM WHEREVER THEY GO.

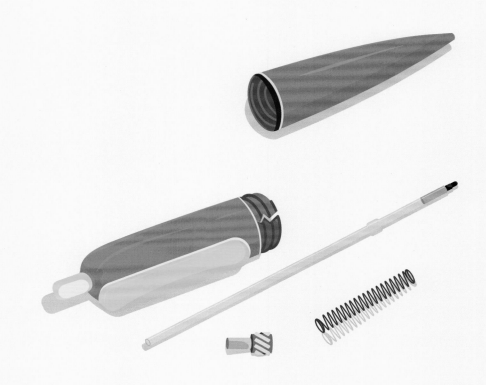

CLICK...

CLICK! CLICK, CLICK! CLICK, CLICK, CLICK!

I SUGGEST YOU PEN-CLICKING PANSIES SHUT UP BEFORE SOMEBODY POPS THAT PEN INTO YOUR DARK ORIFICE. YES, IF YOU'RE THE KIND OF PERSON WHO ENJOYS A LITTLE PEN-CLICKING WHILE YOU THINK, THEN I CAN GUARANTEE THAT SOMEBODY HAS ALREADY IMAGINED YOUR DEATH, AND RECITED THEIR ALIBI.

FLOWER BOMB

OKAY, SO WE UNDERSTAND THAT SOME PEOPLE NATURALLY SMELL LIKE ROSES AND SUNSHINE, WHILE OTHERS SMELL LIKE A DONKEY'S ARMPIT. UNFORTUNATELY THAT'S LIFE AND THERE'S NOT MUCH THAT CAN BE DONE. BUT I THINK WE ALL AGREE THAT WE'D RATHER SIT NEXT TO SOMEONE WHO SMELLS LIKE A TROLL'S TOENAIL OVER SOMEONE WHO SMELLS LIKE A FLOWERY CHEMICAL EXPLOSION.

IT'S CALLED A SPRAY BOTTLE, NOT A SHOWER BOTTLE. GET IT RIGHT, FOLKS!

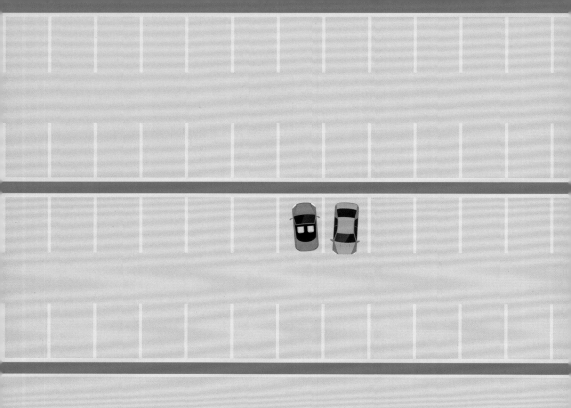

BUMPER BUDDIES

YOU PULL INTO A SUPERMARKET CARPARK ON YOUR MISSION TO SPEAK TO THE MANAGER AND YOU PARK NEXT TO ANOTHER CAR... ONLY, THERE IS ONLY ONE OTHER CAR IN THE ENTIRE CARPARK. ARE YOU INSANE? THERE'S NOTHING WORSE THAN A SPACE INVADER. IF THIS IS YOU THEN IT'S JUSTIFIED TO HAVE YOUR CAR TOWED AND CRUSHED.

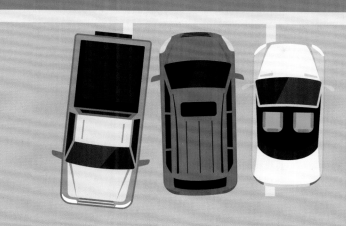

A FINE LINE

SO YOU PARKED NEXT TO SOMEBODY AND ALREADY
RUINED THEIR MORNING, BUT THAT'S NOT ALL! ON
YOUR PARKING ADVENTURES, YOU PARKED AS CLOSE
TO THE WHITE LINE AS YOU CAN POSSIBLY GET AND
NOW THE POOR SOD HAS TO CLAMBER THROUGH THE
PASSENGER SIDE JUST TO GO HOME. ANY CLOSER AND I
CAN ASSURE YOU, YOU'RE MORE PSYCHOTIC THAN THE
WARDENS ISSUING YOU A FINE!

YOU'RE SLURPED!

SIPPING, SLURPING, PSYCHOPATHS.

IF YOU CAN HEAR OVER THE SLURPING OF YOUR DRINK, YOU MIGHT NOTICE THE GROANING AND SIGHING OF THOSE AROUND YOU – YOU'RE AT THE TOP OF THEIR HATE LIST, WITH YOUR SQUEAKY STRAW AND EMPTY CUP... IF YOU WANT TO KEEP YOUR FRIENDS, THE TIME TO ACT IS NOW!

PUT DOWN THE CUP NOW – TO PRESERVE EVERYONE'S SANITY AND TO KEEP YOU FROM SLURPING YOUR WAY INTO AN UNSOLVED CRIME DOCUMENTARY!

SNAP, CRACKLE AND POP

DID YOU MAKE EYE CONTACT WITH SOMEONE, AND ALL
OF A SUDDEN HEAR A DISTINCT SNAP? THAT STOMACH-
CHURNING, BLOOD-CURDLING CREAKING OF BONES ONLY
MEANS ONE THING... THEY'VE SNAPPED THEIR NECK! NOT
ONLY DOES IT MAKE YOU FEEL SICK, THEY ALSO MADE
IT ONTO A SCENE FROM JAMES WAN'S LATEST MOVIE!

O.C.DISHES

YOU'VE HEARD THE SAYING 'THERE'S A PLACE FOR EVERYTHING AND EVERYTHING IN ITS PLACE'. WELL, KITCHENS HAVE A KIND OF ORDER THAT MUST BE MAINTAINED AT ALL COSTS. IT TAKES ONE SECOND OF YOUR DAY TO TAKE AN OBJECT AND PUT IT BACK WHERE IT BELONGS, BUT SOME MONSTERS JUST LOVE TO SEE DISRUPTION WHEREVER THEY GO. SPOONS LIKE TO SIT WITH THEIR FRIENDS, FORKS HAVE FAMILY TOO, AND KNIVES CARE WHERE THEY'RE KEPT...

TAKING THE PEE

YOU PAID OVER £10 TO WATCH A MOVIE, NOT VISIT
THE BOG! IF YOU'RE THE INCONVENIENT BEING WHO
HAS TO STAND UP MID-MOVIE, ADDING A SHADOW INTO
SOMEONE'S ILLEGAL RECORDING OF THE SAME FILM,
THEN SHUFFLING SLOWLY TO THE END OF YOUR ROW
BEFORE CREAKING THE CINEMA DOOR OPEN, THEN DAY
RELEASE IS OVER AND YOU SHOULD GO BACK TO YOUR
PADDED CELL AT ONCE!

SIP AND SLIDE

DRINKING TEA CAN BE A SIPPERY SLOPE INTO
PSYCHOSIS. ONE MINUTE YOU CAN BE DOWNING
YOUR DRINK, AND THE NEXT YOU'RE ASKING FOR A
FRESH CUP OF TEA AFTER LEAVING HALF OF YOUR
CURRENT ONE. THIS ISN'T A HALF EMPTY, HALF FULL
SITUATION, THIS IS ABOUT WASTING PRECIOUS TEA...

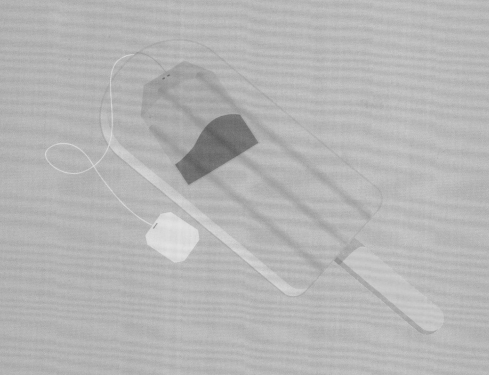

COLD BREWED KILLERS

WHAT'S A GREAT DEAL WORSE THOUGH, IS THAT SOME
LUNATICS WILL FORGET ALL ABOUT THEIR NICE HOT
CUPPA UNTIL IT GOES STONE COLD, THEN WHEN THEY
FINALLY REMEMBER IT EXISTS, THEY WILL CHUG OFF
THIS ICE COLD BEVERAGE LIKE IT'S NORMAL!

THE PENNY DROPPED

WHO ARE YOU PEOPLE, WALKING AROUND WITH BULKY WALLETS LIKE IT'S THE 1700S? SPARE CHANGE IS FOR THE WEAK! IF YOU'RE GOING TO PAY FOR £20 WORTH OF ITEMS WITH A HANDFUL OF 5, 10 AND 20 PENCE PIECES, THEN YOU DESERVE WHATEVER ABUSE THE CASHIER THROWS AT YOU. EVER HEARD OF A DEBIT CARD? JEEEZ!

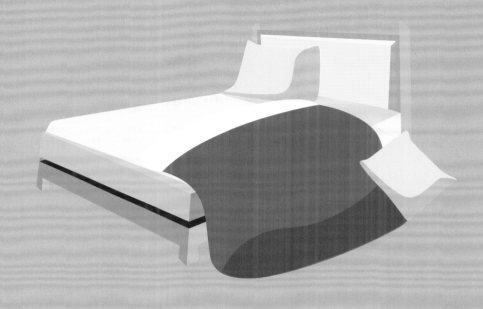

A LOAD OF SHEET

YOU WAKE UP AND LEAVE THE HOUSE WITHOUT MAKING YOUR BED... WHAT ON EARTH IS WRONG WITH YOU!? HOW ARE YOU SUPPOSED TO CRAWL INTO BED TONIGHT, KNOWING YOUR SHEETS ARE ALL CRINKLED AND TWISTED, PILLOWS FLAT AS A FART, IN AN UNBELIEVABLE ACT OF DISORDER? DON'T YOU KNOW HOW TO MAKE A BED, OR IS IT THAT YOU LIKE THE DISHEVELLED LIFESTYLE? HONESTLY...

HOW DO YOU EXPECT TO PULL IF YOUR SHEETS CAN'T ACT THE PART?

SPACE INVADER

YOU'RE DECIDING WHICH POT NOODLE YOU WANT TO BUY FOR LUNCH AND YOUR INTERNAL INTRUDER ALARM GOES OFF... THERE'S SOMEBODY BEHIND YOU. BUT NOT JUST BEHIND YOU, THEY'VE ENTERED YOUR PERSONAL SPACE... THIS, MY FRIENDS, IS A SPACE INVADER! IT'S NOT ONLY CONSIDERED EXTREMELY RUDE AND CREEPY TO ENTER SOMEONE'S PERSONAL SPACE, IT'S ALSO EXTREMELY PSYCHOTIC!

LOON-E - PHONE HOME

IT'S NORMAL TO GET OVERLY EXCITED AND LOUD WHILE ON THE PHONE (IF YOU SEE A CUTE PUPPY, YOU'RE PROBABLY GOING TO SQUEAL IN DELIGHT), BUT WHEN DOES IT BECOME PSYCHOTIC? PERHAPS WHEN YOUR CONVERSATIONS STOP BEING ALL "HEY THERE, WANT TO GO FOR COFFEE LATER?", AND MORE LIKE "YES I'LL COME, WHAT TIME? I REALLY WANT A LATTE!!!!". KNOW THE DIFFERENCE. STOP BEING A WEIRDO AND PRACTICE YOUR SOCIAL SKILLS.

SPEED FREAK

THERE'S ALWAYS THAT ONE DRIVER — THEY PULL OUT RIGHT IN FRONT OF YOU AT THE SPEED OF LIGHT (ALMOST FORCING YOU TO EMERGENCY BRAKE), THEN THEY SLOW DOWN TO A SNAIL'S PACE. BREAKING THE SPEED LIMIT IS BAD, BUT NOBODY ASKED FOR YOU TO DO 20 ON A 40 ROAD! BUT THEN, IN A STRANGE TURN OF EVENTS, THE SAME DRIVER SUDDENLY REALISES IT'S A 40 ROAD, AND CHOOSES TO GO 55 PAST EVERY SPEED CAMERA THEY SPOT. WHAT AN ABSOLUTE NUTTER!

MOVIE MIGHT

YOU SETTLE DOWN TO WATCH A MOVIE. A MOVIE YOUR
FRIEND VERY SPECIFICALLY SAID THEY WANTED TO
WATCH. YOU'VE HEARD THEM TALK ABOUT THEIR CAT,
THE PRICE OF BANANAS GOING UP, AND ASKING WHO
THE MAIN CHARACTER IS 15 TIMES - AND YOU'RE ONLY
5 MINUTES IN!

YOU HAVE AN HOUR AND A HALF TO GO BEFORE THE
ENDING CREDITS, NEXT TIME MAYBE YOU'LL THINK
TWICE ABOUT WATCHING A MOVIE WITH A CHATTY
PSYCHO LIKE THIS ONE. MAYBE TRY SWITCHING ON THE
SUBTITLES, IT MIGHT HELP!

CRUNCH!

YOU COULD BE A SWEET OLD LADY, WITH WISE WRINKLES AND A SMILE THAT MELTS BUTTER – BUT AS SOON AS YOU START CRUNCHING THOSE CRISPS, YOU BECOME THE DEVIL HIMSELF!

THESE KIND OF MANIACS TARGET QUIET SPACES LIKE OFFICES, CINEMAS AND LIBRARIES. THEY FIND THE PERFECT SPACE (USUALLY SOMEWHERE ECHOEY OR RIGHT BESIDE YOU) AND THEN THEY MAKE THEIR MOVE. CRUNCH. CRUNCH. CRUNCH. TESTING THE PATIENCE OF EVEN THE MOST TOLERANT PEOPLE, HOPING TO SEND THEM INTO AN UNMANAGEABLE RAGE!

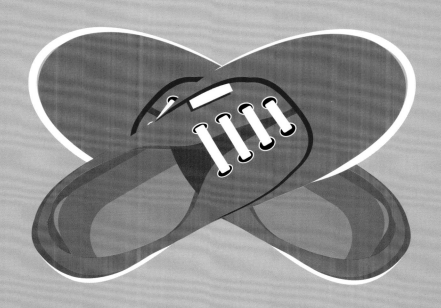

SHOE AWAY!

IF YOU'RE THE KIND OF PERSON WHO KICKS OFF THEIR
SHOES AND DOESN'T PUT THEM STRAIGHT AND TIDY,
THEN YOU DESERVE FOR SOMEONE TO PINCH THOSE
SAME SHOES AND KICK YOU IN THE SHINS WITH THEM!
SERIOUSLY, HOW HARD IS IT TO PUT TWO SHOES NEXT
TO EACH OTHER? ARE YOU WAITING FOR SOMEONE TO
FALL AND BREAK THEIR NECK? - AT LEAST CHECK TO
SEE IF THEY HAVE LIFE INSURANCE FIRST!

ODD BALL

THERE ARE SOME DISGUSTING PEOPLE IN THE WORLD WHO ARE CAPABLE OF HORRIFIC THINGS LIKE WEARING ODD SOCKS - ON PURPOSE! YES, WE KNOW YOU EXIST, YOU FOUL CREATURES...

YOU COME MARCHING IN, WEARING SPOTS AND STRIPES, LOOKING LIKE A DEFORMED MR.TUMBLE. WHEN WILL YOU REALISE THAT SOCKS COME IN PAIRS FOR A REASON? IT'S A PHASE, SON. TIME TO PULL UP YOUR BIG BOY SOCKS.

CRUNCHY NUTTER

THERE ARE TWO KINDS OF CRISP EATERS IN THE WORLD. THOSE WHO EAT A FULL BAG LIKE YOU'RE SUPPOSED TO, AND THOSE WHO WILL HAPPILY LEAVE HALF A BAG OF CRISPS FOR LATER, ON THE BASIS OF BEING 'FULL'. NO, YOU CAN'T BE FULL FROM EATING 4 SLICES OF POTATO, STOP FOOLING YOURSELF.

BUT THIS KIND OF PERSON WON'T HAVE ANY OF IT. THEY'LL SIT THERE, STAPLING UP A BAG OF READY SALTED WALKERS LIKE IT'S A THREE COURSE MEAL. THIS HALF BAG WILL LAST THEM FOR AT LEAST TWO MORE SITTINGS. WHAT A FREAK!

PILES OF PILLOWS

THERE ARE TWO KINDS OF PEOPLE IN THIS WORLD. THOSE WHO SIT ON A CHAIR OR SOFA NORMALLY, AND THOSE WHO SIT ON THE CUSHIONS AS THOUGH THEY HAVE A BOTTOM FULL OF HAEMORRHOIDS. IF YOUR SETTEE IS REALLY THAT UNCOMFORTABLE, PERHAPS YOU SHOULD INVEST IN A NEW ONE, BUT FOR THE LOVE OF GOD, GROW UP AND STOP ACTING LIKE A PILE INFESTED WEIRDO!

SNOT THE WAY TO GO

THERE'S ONE KIND OF PSYCHOPATH OUT THERE
THAT REALLY SHOULDN'T BE LET INTO SOCIETY –
PHLEGM SPITTERS! YOU'RE WALKING DOWN THE ROAD,
MINDING YOUR OWN BUSINESS, WHEN A CREEP WITH
SNOT IN THEIR CHEST DECIDES THAT TODAY'S THE
DAY THEY WANT TO RELEASE THEIR THROAT BOGIES
INTO THE WORLD.

IF YOU'RE THIS PERSON, THEN SHAME ON YOU!
LITTERING THE STREETS WITH MANKY MUCUS REALLY
ISN'T THE WAY TO GO IF YOU WANT TO KEEP YOUR
FRIENDS.

GRANTED, THERE'S A RARE SPECIES OF NUTTER
THAT'S WORSE THAN YOU, AND THAT'S PEOPLE
WHO HAVE THE DISGUSTING ABILITY TO SHOOT
SNOT OUT OF THEIR NOSE AND ONTO THE PAVEMENT
BESIDE THEM – NO HANDS NECESSARY!

A RECIPE FOR DISASTER

DENNIS HAS A CHICKEN WRAP, TONY HAS A CHEESE SANDWICH AND SANDRA HAS A SALAD. WAIT, WHAT'S THAT? YOU HAVE A... A... FISH?!?!

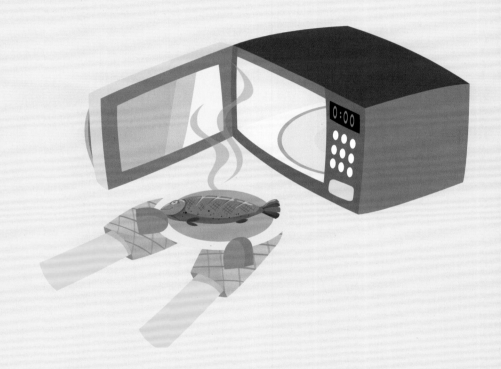

LUNCHTIME IN THE OFFICE IS A THING TO BE FEARED. THERE'S ALWAYS THAT ONE PERSON WHO HAS NO CONSIDERATION FOR THEIR COLLEAGUES, BRINGING IN THEIR TROUT OR KIPPERS AND WARMING THEM UP IN THE COMMUNAL MICROWAVE. WHAT A SICK INDIVIDUAL THEY MUST BE TO WANT TO PURPOSELY GAS THEIR WORKMATES WITH FISHY FUMES. BLERGH!

SECTION THE SQUEAK

SQUEAK, SQUEAK, SQUEAK... THERE'S ALWAYS THAT ONE PERSON, WALKING THROUGH A QUIET ROOM (USUALLY AN OFFICE OR LIBRARY) SQUEAKY SHOES IN TOW. SURELY YOU'RE NOT OBLIVIOUS TO THE METAPHORICAL MICE IN YOUR HEELS. DO YOU LIKE 'ACCIDENTALLY' BREAKING THE UNWRITTEN RULE OF SILENCE IN LIBRARIES?

YOU'RE EITHER A REBEL OR A PSYCHO, THAT MUCH IS FOR CERTAIN!

TAP, TAP, TAP

TAP, TAP, TAP, TAPPING ON A TABLE IS ONE THING
THAT WILL MAKE YOU A TARGET FOR VIOLENCE, AND
NOBODY IF SO, WILL SAVE YOU. IT WOULDN'T BE SO
BAD IF WE KNEW WHAT TUNE YOU'RE TAPPING ALONG
TO, BUT CONSIDERING THE TUNE IS IN YOUR MIND, WE
CAN ONLY WONDER...

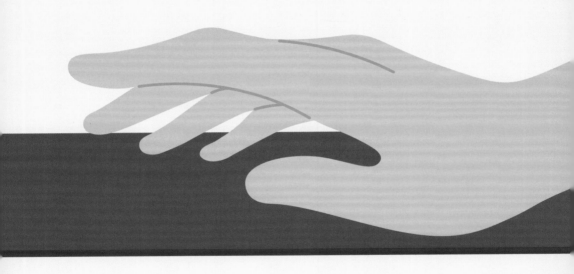

LIKE A TAP DRIPPING IN AN EMPTY ROOM, IT'S NO
WONDER YOU'VE GOT A SCREW LOOSE.

A TANG OF MADNESS

BELIEVE IT OR NOT, THERE'S A WRONG WAY TO DRINK ORANGE JUICE... NORMAL PEOPLE WOULDN'T DREAM OF DOING IT, BUT THERE ARE SOME DISTURBED SOULS IN THE WORLD WHO DELIBERATELY BRUSH THEIR TEETH WITH MINTY FRESH TOOTHPASTE BEFORE TAKING A GULP OF ORANGE.

DOES IT TASTE NICE? HELL NO. DO THEY DO IT ANYWAY? YOU CAN BET YOUR DAY RELEASE THEY DO!

A BIT FISHY

IF YOU ORDER A TUNA SANDWICH FROM A CAFÉ, YOU'RE
NOT A PSYCHO, JUST A BIT OF AN IDIOT. BUT IF YOU
THEN PROCEED TO SIT ON A BUSY TRAIN AND PULL
OUT YOUR WARM, SWEATY TUNA SANDWICH, THEN YOU
DESERVE TO BE TIED UP AND MADE TO GO SWIMMING
WITH THE FISH!

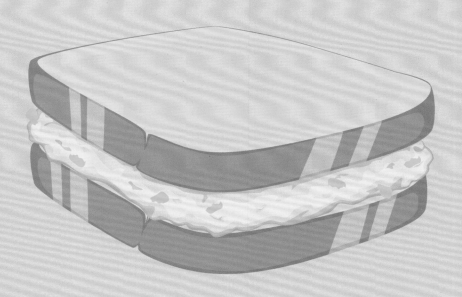

IT SMELLS ROTTEN AT THE BEST OF TIMES, SO WHEN
YOU POLLUTE THE UNVENTILATED TUBE WITH YOUR
FISHY SCENTS, YOU'RE GOING TO MAKE ENEMIES FAST!

NAILED IT!

CHOMPING AND CRUNCHING YOUR NAILS AND HANGNAILS IS SOMETHING TO BE ASHAMED OF. THERE ARE CLIPPERS DESIGNED FOR THIS EXACT ISSUE - USE THEM! IMAGINE TALKING TO SOMEONE AND THEY JUST DECIDE TO SNAP OFF A BIT OF NAIL WITH THEIR TEETH AND START CHEWING IT. YOU'RE BASICALLY EATING YOURSELF, YOU CANNIBAL!

CRAZED AND CRUNCHY

THE 'SHREDDIES NANNIES' WOULD BE
HEARTBROKEN TO HEAR THAT SOME CRAZED LOONS
CAN'T EVEN BE BOTHERED TO POUR MILK ON
THEIR KNITTED CREATIONS...

SERIOUSLY, HOW DO THEY LIVE THEIR LIVES,
KNOWING THEY EAT CEREAL AS DRY AS A BONE?
ESPECIALLY FOR THE LIKES OF WEETABIX AND
SHREDDED WHEAT! EVEN POURING WATER OVER
THEM WOULD BE AN IMPROVEMENT...

YOU'RE LAGGING OUT

SO YOU'RE WATCHING A MOVIE, AND THE MAIN ANTAGONIST IS LAYING ON THE FLOOR, LIVING THE LAST MOMENTS OF THEIR LIFE. THE SOUND HOWEVER, IS STILL THINKING ABOUT CATCHING UP, AND THE HERO OF THE MOVIE IS CONFESSING THEIR LOVE!? HOW DO YOU PSYCHOPATHS DEAL WITH THIS LAG? YOU MUST BE COMPLETELY SCREWY TO SIT THROUGH 2 AND A HALF HOURS OF BUFFERING, LAG, AND UNSYNCED SOUND... AND STILL ENJOY IT!

SPREAD IT!

THERE'S THAT ONE PERSON IN THE OFFICE WHO LIKES SPREADSHEETS A LITTLE TOO MUCH. THEY DREAM ABOUT THEM, FANTASISING ABOUT THEIR PERFECTLY ALIGNED COLUMNS AND VLOOKUPS THAT CAN DO PRACTICALLY ANYTHING... THEY BECOME ECSTATIC WHEN THEY SEE A COLOUR CO-ORDINATED PIVOT TABLE...

THE REALITY IS, THEY'RE LIVING IN A FANTASY WORLD, SEEING THINGS THAT AREN'T REALLY THERE... THEY'RE INSANE! EVERYONE KNOWS SPREADSHEETS ARE HARDLY BEARABLE AT THE BEST OF TIMES.

SHARPEN UP

PILES OF PENCIL LEAD AND WOOD SCATTERED ON YOUR
DESK AND AROUND THE DUSTBIN. WHAT ARE YOU,
A CHILD? GROW SOME BALLS AND GET YOURSELF A
BALLPOINT PEN! WE'RE NOT ASKING FOR THE WORLD - OR
EVEN AN INK AND QUILL...

WOULD YOU SIGN YOUR WILL WITH A PENCIL? WHAT ABOUT
YOUR MARRIAGE CERTIFICATE? I DIDN'T THINK SO...

LIVE, LAUGH, LOCKED UP

IT'S NOT 2009 ANYMORE, SO STOP LIVING IN THE PAST. THE TIME FOR 'LIVE, LAUGH, LOVE' SIGNS IS OVER. IF YOU CAN'T BEAR TO LET GO OF YOUR HEART PLAQUES AND WALL STICKERS, THEN YOU HAVE ISSUES (AND IT'S NOT FINDING MORE WALL SPACE). YOU'RE A BIT OF AN ODDBALL, STUCK IN A PURGATORY OF PILLOWS, LIGHTBOXES AND CANDLES, ALL DECORATED WITH CHEESY LIFE QUOTES AND TRASHY GLITTER.

STORE YOUR SANITY

IF YOUR HOME DOESN'T HAVE AT LEAST ONE JUNK DRAWER, THEN SURELY YOU MUST LIVE IN A PADDED CELL INSTEAD.

JUNK DRAWERS AREN'T JUST A THING OF CONVENIENCE, THEY SHOW THAT YOU HAVE YOUR SANITY INTACT. SERIOUSLY, WHAT ELSE COULD YOU POSSIBLY KEEP IN THAT KITCHEN DRAWER? ORGANISED CUTLERY? NEATLY LABELLED HERBS AND SPICES?! NO WAY! GET YOUR LIFE SORTED OUT AND MAKE YOURSELF A JUNK DRAWER!

A BIT TOWELLED

AFTER JUST FINISHING YOUR SPAG BOL, YOU PICK UP
THE NICE WHITE TEA TOWEL AND WIPE YOUR FACE...
CONGRATULATIONS, YOU'RE GOING TO HELL!

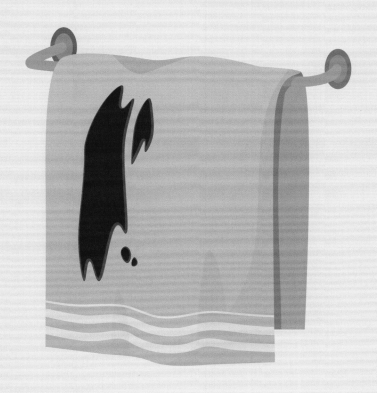

NOT ONLY HAVE YOU MUTILATED AND PERMANENTLY
STAINED A DECENT TOWEL, YOU'VE ALSO HINDERED THE
DISH WASHING PROCESS! NOW YOU NEED TO GO FETCH
ANOTHER TOWEL - WHICH IS SURE TO BECOME YOUR
NEXT VICTIM...

STAMPED AND SIGNED FOR

ARE STAMP COLLECTORS HIDING SOMETHING A LITTLE MORE INSIDIOUS? YOU CAN'T JUST COLLECT TINY PICTURES OF THE QUEEN'S HEAD AND NOT LOOK SUSPICIOUS... IS THIS THE BEGINNING OF A CRIME DOCUMENTARY? IT USUALLY STARTS WITH FRYING ANTS WITH A MAGNIFYING GLASS, BUT ANYTHING IS POSSIBLE THESE DAYS...

FISHING FOR CONDIMENTS

THERE'S ONE THING IN LIFE THAT CAN MAKE THE TOUGHEST INDIVIDUALS GAG... FOOD STUCK IN THE PLUGHOLE. IF YOU DON'T LOOK LIKE E.T. WHEN FISHING OUT THAT SOGGY SPAGHETTI OR MOIST MUSHROOM, THEN WE HAVE CAUSE TO BELIEVE YOU'RE A LITTLE TAPPED IN THE HEAD (PUN INTENDED...).

FREAKY FANS

IT'S SNOWING OUTSIDE, YOU HAVE A FAUX FUR
BLANKET WRAPPED AROUND YOU, AND YET YOU STILL
INSIST THAT A FAN BE TURNED ON! ARE YOU INSANE?
YOU CAN'T POSSIBLY BE TOO WARM — BUT EVEN IF YOU
WERE, JUST OPEN A WINDOW A LITTLE AND LET THE
FROSTY AIR TICKLE YOUR TOES FOR A BIT.

GINGER NUTTY

THERE'S NOTHING WORSE THAN A SOGGY BISCUIT
FLOATING IN YOUR BREW. NOW, WE'RE NOT SAYING
THERE'S ANYTHING WRONG WITH DUNKING YOUR
BICCIES, BUT IF YOU'RE GOING TO RISK DOUBLE
DIPPING, THEN YOU SHOULD BE PREPARED TO POUR
YOUR CUPPA AWAY IF YOUR DIGESTIVE BREAKS (LIKE
THAT SCENE IN THE TITANIC WHEN JACK LETS GO...).

SOME FERAL PEOPLE ACTUALLY THINK THAT DRINKING
A CRUMB INFESTED BREWAGE IS ACCEPTABLE. NAY MY
FRIEND. DOWN THE DRAIN IT GOES!

NO FRIES ON ME!

SO YOU ORDER YOURSELF A CHEEKY MACCIES. YOU MIGHT BE A CHICKEN NUGGET KIND OF CRAZY – THE KIND WHO ORDERS TWO 20 NUGGET SHARE BOXES ALL TO THEMSELVES. THAT'S ACCEPTABLE AND ACTUALLY QUITE UNDERSTANDABLE.

BUT THEN THERE'S THE OTHER TYPE OF CRAZY... YOU KNOW IT, THE FRIES AND MILKSHAKE KIND. THE KIND OF PSYCHO WHO HAPPILY MIXES THEIR FOOD AND DRINK TOGETHER, THE SALTY GOODNESS OF FRIES WITH THE THICK SLUSH OF A MILKSHAKE. EWW.

JUST SCRAPED SANITY

IF YOU DON'T TURN INTO A SHIVERY, CRINGY MESS
WHENEVER A CHALKBOARD IS SCREECHED, THEN YOU'RE
EITHER DEAF OR A STONE COLD PSYCHO.

IF THAT ISN'T BAD ENOUGH, THERE'S PEOPLE (FOR
LACK OF A BETTER WORD) IN THIS WORLD WHO
PURPOSELY SCRAPE THEIR NAILS DOWN CHALKBOARDS
FOR FUN! THESE FERAL ANIMALS SHOULD BE LOCKED
AWAY FOR OUR OWN PROTECTION!

DROPPED AND DISTURBED

SOME PEOPLE ARE JUST BORN TO LIVE LIFE ON THE EDGE
AND WILL WALK AROUND, PHONE IN HAND AND NO PHONE
CASE IN SIGHT. THEY JUST TRUST THEMSELVES NOT TO
DROP AND SMASH THEIR SCREEN (HOW WILD IS THAT?!).
WE'RE NOT SURE IF THEY'RE BRAVE OR BEZERK, BUT WE
DO KNOW THAT WE'D RATHER NOT RISK IT!

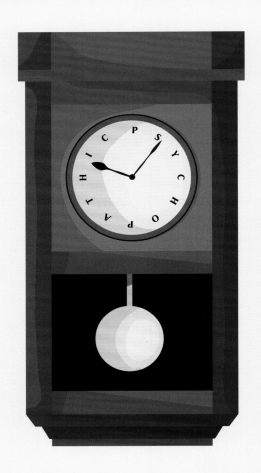

WHAT MAKES YOU TICK?

TICK, TICK, TICK, TICK... IT'S ENOUGH TO BRING ANYONE TO INSANITY. PERHAPS THAT'S WHY SOME STRANGE PEOPLE FIND IT EASY – AND SOMETIMES EVEN BETTER – TO SLEEP WITH A CLOCK IN THEIR ROOM.

IT'S ALMOST A FORM OF SOUND TORTURE OR HYPNOSIS TO THE MIND.

WHAT A CHILLER

THE TEMPERATURE IS BELOW 0 DEGREES. ICICLES ARE FORMING ON THE TIP OF YOUR NOSE AND YOU LOOK LIKE A DRAGON WHEN YOU BREATHE.

HOW WOULD YOU DEAL WITH IT? WOULD YOU POP THE HEATING ON LIKE A NORMAL MEMBER OF SOCIETY, OR ARE YOU THAT KIND OF PERSON? YOU KNOW THE ONE – "PUT A JUMPER ON, IT'S NOT COLD ENOUGH FOR HEATING"... THE WORST KIND OF PERSON.

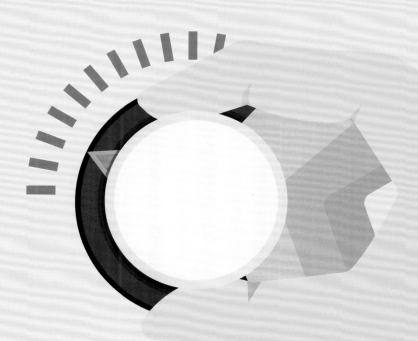

BONKERS BOGIES

THERE'S NOTHING WORSE THAN WITNESSING SOMEBODY
PICK A STRINGY, GLOOPY BOGEY OUT OF THEIR NOSE
AND THEN LICK IT OFF THEIR FINGER. YOU CALL THEM
OUT FOR THIS HORRIFIC ACT, BUT THEY DENY IT –
"YOU SAW WRONG", "I WAS SCRATCHING THE OUTSIDE",
"MIND YOUR OWN BUSINESS".

YOU OFFER THEM A TISSUE OR HANKIE TO HELP CLEAR
THEIR NOSE OF SNOT AND GUNK, BUT THEY DECLINE.

WHAT A SHAMEFUL ACT.

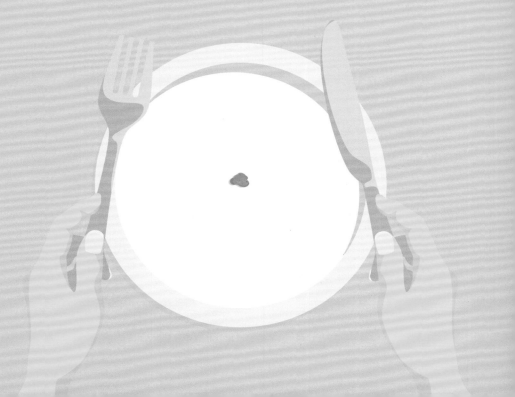

ERRATIC EARWAX

WHILE WE'RE ALREADY TALKING ABOUT PICKING THINGS OUT OF ORIFICES, WHAT ABOUT THOSE LUNATICS WHO PICK THEIR EARWAX AND EAT IT? SURELY THEY CAN'T LIKE THE BITTER, SOUR TASTE OF EAR GUNK! EWW!

(P.S. DON'T STICK US IN THE SAME CATEGORY AS THESE NUTCASES, WE HAD TO GOOGLE THE TASTE!)

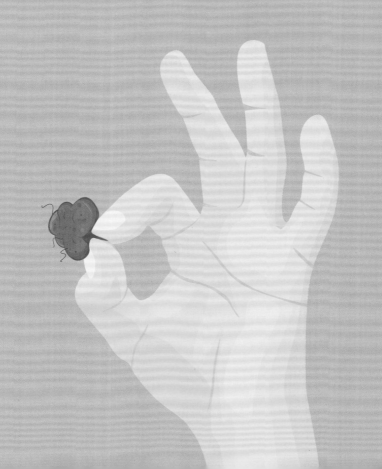

DELIRIOUS DISHES

IT'S TIME FOR ANOTHER BREW-ROUND, AND LET'S FACE IT, YOU'RE EITHER THE PERSON WITH A FAIRLY CLEAN MUG, OR THE PERSON WHOSE MUG HASN'T SEEN DISH SOAP IN 4 YEARS.

IF YOU'RE THE LATTER, THEN WHY?! I'M SURPRISED YOU EVEN HAVE A MUG LEFT WITH ALL THAT BUILD-UP. IT WOULD MAKE A GREAT WARNING LABEL THOUGH... LOOKING LIKE A LUNG FROM A CIGARETTE PACKET!

WHAT COLOUR IS YOUR MUG AGAIN?

GREEN LIGHT, RED FLAG

YOU GET TO THE CROSSING AND PRESS THE BUTTON. GREAT! A PEDESTRIAN ACTUALLY USING A PEDESTRIAN CROSSING! BUT WAIT… OF COURSE IT'S TOO GOOD TO BE TRUE. THEY'RE ALREADY ACROSS THE ROAD AND THE LIGHTS HAVE JUST TURNED RED. YOU JUST WITNESSED A PSYCHOPATH DOING WHAT THEY DO BEST.

IF YOU DO THIS, THEN YOU OBVIOUSLY DON'T DRIVE A CAR, BECAUSE IF YOU DID, YOU'D SEE HOW ANNOYING YOU ARE!

FASHIONABLY INSANE

SO YOU'RE SPORTING A NIRVANA TEE TODAY. AWESOME!
IF YOU'RE A NORMIE, THEN YOU KNOW HOW COOL THIS
GRUNGE BAND REALLY IS, BUT IF YOU'RE A LITTLE
BIT TWISTED, YOU'LL BE BRAGGING TO YOUR FRIENDS
ABOUT THIS AWESOME NEW CLOTHING BRAND YOU'VE
COME ACROSS - YOU KNOW, WITH THAT FAMOUS FASHION
DESIGNER KURT COBAIN...

A BIT BUMPED

SO YOU'RE DRIVING BEHIND A REALLY SLOW NISSAN
MICRA, AND THEN YOU SEE IT — THE 'I LOVE MY DOG
MORE THAN I LOVE MY HUSBAND' BUMPER STICKER.
YES, IT'S A LITTLE PENSIONER LADY DRIVING THAT
CAR... AND THE MORE YOU LOOK, THE MORE STICKERS
YOU FIND... 'RIP PAUL WALKER', 'POWERED BY FAIRY
DUST', 'CHEESUS LOVES YOU'. THESE KIND OF PEOPLE
ARE ON THE SAME INSANITY LEVEL AS THOSE WHO GIVE
THEIR CARS EYELASHES...

PUMP UP THE JAM

DO YOU LIKE TO PLAY PETROL ROULETTE? YOU PULL
THE PUMP TRIGGER AND TRY TO STOP IT AT THE RIGHT
MOMENT — A £20, £30... IT'S A GAME ALL DRIVERS
LIKE TO PLAY. THAT IS, ALL 'NORMAL' DRIVERS. IF
YOU'RE A WACKO, YOU PROBABLY STOP THE TRIGGER AT
£17.38 OR SOME DIRTY NUMBER LIKE THAT!

GET YOUR BRAIN CHECKED!

TOPPED UP SCREWBALL

THERE'S NOTHING WORSE THAN SOMEBODY WHO GOES
UP TO THE BAR IN A PUB AND ASKS FOR THEIR HALF
EMPTY PINT OF NOW-WARM LAGER TO BE 'TOPPED-UP'.
WHAT'S WRONG WITH YOU PEOPLE?! HOW HAVE YOU NOT
BEEN THROWN OUT AND BARRED FOR LIFE BY NOW? DOWN
IT ALL LIKE THE BEAST YOU ARE AND STOP BEING A
FRUIT LOOP!

SWEET BUT PSYCHO

CHOCCY FOR BREAKY... WHAT ARE YOU, FIVE?!

NUTELLA ON A CHOCOLATE SCONE PERHAPS? MAYBE A
CHOCOLATE BAR SANDWICH? AT THIS POINT, WE'RE
ONLY WONDERING ONE THING – HOW ARE YOUR TEETH
STILL INTACT? YOUR INSANITY LEVELS WILL SOON BE
RIGHT UP THERE ALONGSIDE YOUR SUGAR LEVELS!

HAM AND P-P-PINEAPPLE!

YOU'RE ORDERING PIZZA FOR YOU AND YOUR PALS AND SOMEONE SUGGESTS HAM AND PINEAPPLE. HOLD UP!

WHAT KIND OF PERSON WOULD EVEN LET THAT ESCAPE THEIR MOUTH? A PSYCHO, THAT'S WHO. AND NOT JUST ANY PSYCHO EITHER, BUT ONE THAT HAS NO REMORSE FOR RUINING EVERYONE'S APPETITE. EVEN ITALIANS (THE INVENTORS OF THE SACRED PIZZA), ARE DISGUSTED BY PINEAPPLE'S PRESENCE!

PUDDLED

IT'S RAINING, IT'S POURING,
A BIG PUDDLE IS FORMING...

YOU KNOW WHAT'S NEXT. YOU'RE EITHER THE DERANGED
DRIVER AIMING FOR THE PUDDLE, OR THE POOR SOD
JUST TRYING TO STAY DRY. IF YOU'RE THE DRIVER,
WELL SHAME ON YOU. I HOPE YOU STEP IN SOMETHING
WET EVERY TIME YOU WEAR SOCKS AROUND THE HOUSE.

STILL, SPARKLING, OR TAPPED?

LOOK, EVERYONE NEEDS TO STAY HYDRATED... AND I
GUESS THAT ANY WAY TO GET SOME H2O INTO YOUR
BODY IS GOOD. HOWEVER, IF YOU GENUINELY PREFER
SPARKLING WATER TO STILL, YOU NEED TO GIVE YOUR
HEAD A WOBBLE. POURING YOURSELF A BIG GLASS OF
LIQUID STATIC JUST BECAUSE YOU'RE... THIRSTY?
SOUNDS LIKE A PSYCHOPATH TO ME...

GO GREEN

THERE'S A REASON THE OFFICE SUPPLY CUPBOARD HAS AN ABUNDANCE OF GREEN BIROS. EVERYBODY KNOWS IF YOU WRITE IN GREEN, THEN YOU'RE OBSCENE AND SHOULD BE AVOIDED. IF YOU'RE THE TYPE OF PERSON WHO OPENLY CHOOSES TO USE A GREEN BIRO INSTEAD OF A NORMAL COLOUR, THEN WE HAVE ONE QUESTION FOR YOU. DID YOU SIGN YOUR MARRIAGE CERTIFICATE WITH THAT PEN?

YOU'RE BACON ME CRAZY!

DING! THAT'LL BE YOUR BACON - FRESHLY COOKED IN THE... UM... MICROWAVE?

IF THIS RUBBERY THING THAT JUST CAME OUT OF THE MICROWAVE CAN EVEN RESEMBLE BACON, THEN WE'RE ALL DOOMED. THIS SLAB OF SLOPPY MEAT MAKES A GREAT RADIOACTIVE MEAL FOR ANYONE WHO'S CRAZY ENOUGH TO EAT IT. THE REST OF US WILL JUST WAIT TILL THE FRYING PAN WARMS UP.

BONKERZ

PEOPLE WHO U5E A '5' OR 'Z' INZTEAD OF THE
LETTER 'S' REALLY DO NEED THEIR HEADZ CHECKED.
CAN YOU IMAGINE WRITING UP YOUR 3000 WORD
DI55ERTATION OR CV THE WAY PEOPLE NAME THEIR
5HOPZ AND 5TAGE NAME5?

THE LOONY ON THE BUS GOES
'STAND, STAND, STAND'

BUSES ARE COMPLETELY FULL OF SEATS, SO WHY DO SOME CRAZIES REFUSE TO SIT DOWN? THE BUS COULD BE COMPLETELY EMPTY AND SOME WEIRDO WILL STILL BE STOOD UP, SWINGING FROM SIDE TO SIDE WHENEVER IT TURNS A CORNER. THE HANDLES AND POLES ARE FOR WHEN THE BUS IS PACKED, NOT SO YOU CAN PRETEND TO BE FEATURING IN A MUSIC VIDEO – ALL INSIDE YOUR HEAD!

IF YOU'RE THIS PERSON, THEN SIT DOWN, SHUT UP, AND ENJOY THE RIDE!

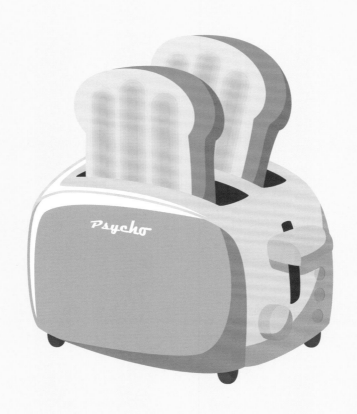

CRUNCHY CRAZIES!

TOAST IS GREAT! BUT ONLY WHEN YOU INCLUDE JAM OR BUTTER TO MOISTEN IT UP. PEOPLE WHO EAT DRY TOAST ARE THE KIND OF PEOPLE YOU NEED TO WORRY ABOUT. IMAGINE WAKING UP THINKING ABOUT ENJOYING SOME DRY, GRITTY, UNMOISTENED TOAST. YOU MIGHT AS WELL EAT CARDBOARD!

PEELING GREAT

WE ALL KNOW THAT ONE PERSON WHO BOUGHT THEMSELVES
A NEW PHONE (THREE MONTHS AGO) AND STILL INSISTS
ON KEEPING THEIR PROTECTIVE FILM ON. IT'S FULL
OF AIR BUBBLES AND SMUDGES BY NOW — BUT THEY'RE
STILL NOT WILLING TO PEEL IT OFF.

DON'T HAVE A FRIEND LIKE THAT? TAKE A LOOK DOWN
AT YOUR OWN PHONE... YOU JUST MIGHT BE THAT PERSON!

EGG-CENTRIC

WHAT CAME FIRST, THE CHICKEN, THE EGG,
OR THE SALMONELLA?

SCRAMBLED EGGS ARE FINE. FRIED EGGS ARE EVEN
BETTER. BUT WHO ON EARTH THOUGHT EATING RAW
EGGS WAS A GOOD IDEA?! WHAT DO YOU DO? MIX THEM
INTO A SMOOTHIE? GULP DOWN THE YOLK IN ONE GO,
HOPING IT GIVES YOU PROTEIN AND NOT AN INTESTINE
INFECTION? SICKENING.

SILENCE OF THE JAMS

YOU GET INTO A CAR AND IT'S DEAD SILENT. NO
MUSIC. NO TALKING. JUST THE SOUND OF THE ENGINE
PURRING, STONES ON THE GROUND BEING FLICKED UP
BY THE TYRES AND THE LOUD TICK TICK TICK OF THE
INDICATOR. ARE YOU HEADED TO A FUNERAL? WHERE'S
THE SOUND? IF THIS IS YOUR CAR THEN YOU'VE GOT
NO EXCUSE. CRANK UP THE VOLUME AND DRIVE LIKE A
HUMAN, NOT A ROBOT.

IF YOU'RE JUST THE PASSENGER THOUGH, THEN YOU
BETTER GRAB HOLD OF YOUR SEATBELT, YOU'RE BEING
DRIVEN BY A CERTIFIED LUNATIC!

GOOD BOY

"C'MERE PAUL", "WHO'S A GOOD GIRL, MARGARET!".

MORE OFTEN THAN NOT, YOU'LL BE WALKING THROUGH A PARK AND HEAR NAMES BEING SHOUTED ACROSS THE GREEN. SOMEBODY MUST HAVE LOST THEIR KID, YOU THINK, BUT AS YOU TURN TO LOOK, YOU SEE A CHIHUAHUA CHASING A GREAT DANE. GREAT. ANOTHER ONE OF THOSE PEOPLE... THE KIND WHO NAMES THEIR PETS AFTER FAMOUS POLITICIANS AND THEIR GREAT AUNTS AND UNCLES.

WHAT A SHAME WE HAVE TO LIVE IN A SOCIETY WHERE PEOPLE LIKE THAT RUN WILD.

ICE AND EASY

IT'S A HOT DAY AND THE ICE-CREAM MAN IS DOING HIS ROUNDS. WHILE EVERYONE LICKS AND SUCKS AT THEIR ICE LOLLIES, YOU'RE BITING INTO YOURS, CRUNCHING THE ICE WITH YOUR TEETH, NOT BATTING AN EYELID. YOU EITHER DON'T FEEL PAIN OR YOU'RE TOO CUCKOO TO CARE. WHERE'S THE BRAIN FREEZE, AND WHY AREN'T YOUR TEETH STINGING?

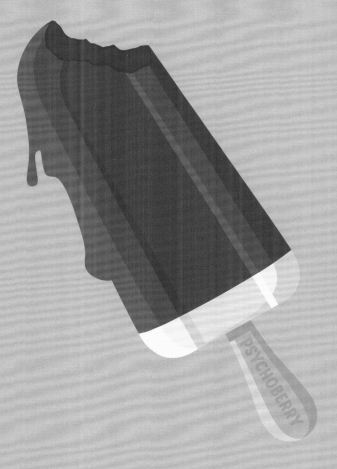

THAT'S NOT MY NAME

SO YOU GAVE BIRTH AND NOW YOU WANT TO NAME THE
LITTLE 'TREASURE'. WHAT YOU NAME YOUR CHILD
CAN HAVE A GREAT IMPACT ON HOW PEOPLE SEE YOUR
MENTAL STATE. IF YOU WANT TO CALL THE LITTLE
BABE SOMETHING LIKE KENNETH, KEITH, OR EVEN
CRAIG, THEN YOU'RE BOUND TO SEE THEM IN A HIGH
VIS AND HARD HAT BY AGE 2.

IF YOU WANT TO BE SUPER EDGY AND NAME THEM
SOMETHING ALONG THE LINES OF BANSHEE OR X Æ
A-XII (YES ELON MUSK, WE'RE TALKING ABOUT YOU
HERE), THEN DO YOURSELF A FAVOUR AND LET YOUR
PARTNER DECIDE INSTEAD.

PICKY PSYCHO

"FULL ENGLISH BREAKFAST PLEASE. NO EGG, NO SAUSAGE, NO RIND ON THE BACON, BEANS WITHOUT THE JUICE, RAW MUSHROOMS AND AN EXTRA HASH BROWN".

DOES THIS SOUND FAMILIAR? YES? IF YOU'RE NOT THE ONE TAKING THE ORDER, THEN YOU MUST BE THE ONE ORDERING... DESPICABLE! CAN'T ANYBODY ORDER A FULL ENGLISH AND IT ACTUALLY BE FULL? THE POOR CHEF HAS TO REMEMBER HOW MANY SINGULAR BEANS YOU WANT – NOT FORGETTING TO KEEP IT SEPARATE FROM YOUR UNCOOKED TOAST! JEEZ, YOU WON'T HAVE THIS ISSUE WHEN YOU GET LOCKED UP FOR BEING A NUTTER, YOU'LL JUST RECEIVE SLOP!

LICK IT SHUT

AWWH, IT'S YOUR GRANNY'S BIRTHDAY! YOU'VE
WRITTEN HER AN ELEGANT BIRTHDAY CARD AND NOW
IT'S TIME TO SEAL THE ENVELOPE... YOU KNOW, YOU
CAN MAKE IT STICK WITHOUT SNOGGING IT SHUT!

THERE'S NOTHING WORSE THAN RECEIVING A DRIPPING
WET CARD, BUT UNFORTUNATELY FOR SOME, ENVELOPE
LICKING IS IN THEIR GENES, AND YOU CAN'T HELP
BUT FEEL SORRY FOR THEM. MAYBE IT'S BEST IF THEY
JUST LEAVE IT OPEN...

DRIVE YOU IN-STAIN

YOU COULD BE THE NICEST PERSON IN THE COUNTRY,
BUT AS SOON AS YOU PUT YOUR MUG ONTO THE SURFACE
WITHOUT PROTECTION, YOU'RE INSTANTLY DEEMED A
LOONY. HOW DARE YOU TOUCH THAT OAK COFFEE TABLE
WITH YOUR NAKED MUG, NO COASTER TO PROTECT IT
FROM HEAT DAMAGE AND TEA STAINS...

SOME PEOPLE DON'T DESERVE NICE THINGS.
YOU'RE ONE OF THEM.

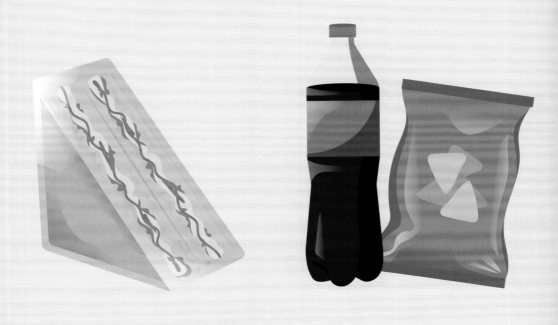

MEAL DEAL MANIAC

YOU GO TO YOUR LOCAL SUPERMARKET ON THE HUNT FOR A NICE, CLASSIC SANDWICH. THIS SITUATION CAN GO TWO WAYS - THE NORMAL WAY, WHERE YOU PICK A DRINK AND A PACKET OF CRISPS TOO AND SAVE YOURSELF A SMALL FORTUNE, OR THE PSYCHOTIC WAY, WHERE YOU COMPLETELY DISREGARD THE MEAL-DEAL OFFER AND GO STRICTLY FOR THE PLAIN CHEESE SANDWICH. IF YOU DO THE LATTER, THEN WHAT KIND OF TWISTED SICKO ARE YOU?

SOCKS AND SAND...ALS

AH YES... PICTURE THIS: YOU'RE ON HOLIDAY,
LISTENING TO THE SOUND OF THE CRASHING WAVES,
SUN SETTING IN THE BACKGROUND, AND FEELING THE
SOFT SAND BETWEEN THE... CREASES OF YOUR NIKES?
SOMETHING NOT SOUND QUITE RIGHT? YOU'RE AT THE
BEACH — TAKE YOUR TRAINERS OFF...
YOU DAMN LUNATIC.

CUCKOO CAKE

IT'S YOUR BIRTHDAY! WHAT A DAY TO CELEBRATE! YOU HOST A PARTY, THERE'S BALLOONS, AND FINGER FOOD, AND EVEN A CAKE!... A CAKE YOU WON'T EVEN HAVE A SLIVER OF.

WHAT'S THE POINT? YOU'RE GETTING OLDER BUT YOU HAVEN'T LOST ALL YOUR TEETH JUST YET, SO WHY RUIN THE DAY BY TURNING YOUR NOSE UP AT CAKE? CAKE, FOR HEAVEN'S SAKE! SOME THINGS SURPRISE ME, BUT THIS REALLY TAKES THE CAKE...

POP!

THERE'S ONE THING MORE TERRIFYING THAN AN AUTOMATIC AIR FRESHENER SQUIRTING IN THE MIDDLE OF THE NIGHT AND THAT'S HEARING A BALLOON POP. YOU KNOW IT'S GOING TO HAPPEN AND YOU STILL END UP JUMPING OUT OF YOUR SKIN. YOU COULD BE HOLDING THE PIN AND YOUR HEART WILL STILL RACE WHEN YOU HEAR THE BANG. WELL, THAT'S MOST PEOPLE. SOME PEOPLE CARRY ON LIKE NOTHING HAPPENED. ARE YOU OKAY? DO YOU HAVE NO FEAR?!

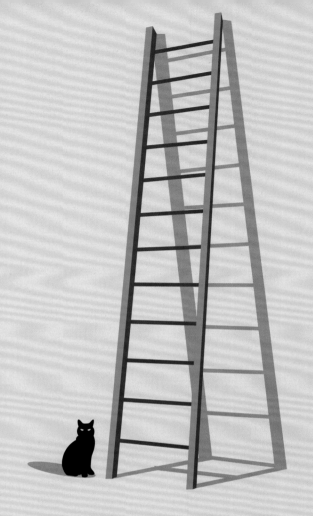

SPOOKY AND KOOKY

SUPERSTITIONS COULD JUST BE THAT, BUT NOBODY IN THEIR RIGHT MIND IS GOING TO TEMPT FATE JUST FOR THE SAKE OF IT. IF YOU DON'T MAKE AN EFFORT TO AVOID WALKING UNDER LADDERS, BREAKING MIRRORS OR WALKING OVER THREE MANHOLES, THEN YOU'RE QUITE FRANKLY ASKING FOR THE CONSEQUENCES!

TOE CAN PLAY AT THAT GAME!

MAKE YOURSELF AT HOME WHY DON'T YOU?

NOBODY CARES WHAT YOU DO IN YOUR OWN HOME — YOU COULD HAVE A SUSAN BOYLE SHRINE IN YOUR LIVING ROOM AND NOBODY WILL BAT AN EYELID (THOUGH THAT'S MORE THAN A LITTLE CREEPY), BUT TO GO INTO ANOTHER PERSON'S HOME AND USE THEIR COFFEE TABLE AS YOUR FOOTSTOOL? GET OUT OF HERE YOU NUTCASE!

ONE FOOT IN THE CUCKOO NEST!

YOU SETTLE DOWN FOR AN EVENING OF SOAP OPERAS ON THE TELLY, AND YOU'RE STILL WEARING YOUR SHOES. YOU'RE NOT PLANNING ON VISITING ALBERT SQUARE OR EMMERDALE FARM, SO WHY ARE YOU STILL WEARING YOUR OUTERWEAR? KICK THOSE SHOES OFF AND LET YOUR FEET BREATHE, BEFORE YOU GET LOCKED UP IN BROADMOOR HOSPITAL!

XOXO

WE UNDERSTAND THAT PUTTING XOXO TO YOUR BOSS
MIGHT GET YOU INTO TROUBLE WITH HR, BUT IT'S
IMPOSSIBLE TO ACCEPT THAT THERE ARE SOME
SCREWBALLS OUT THERE WHO DON'T END THEIR TEXTS
TO THEIR MUMS AND GRANNIES WITH KISSES! HOW
ELSE DO YOU SHOW YOUR LOVE AND APPRECIATION
WHEN YOUR GRANNY ASKS ABOUT YOUR INGROWN
TOENAIL OR YOUR MUM DECLARES THAT DINNER WILL
BE LASAGNE AND GARLIC BREAD?

STOP BEING A PSYCHO AND SHARE THE LOVE!

CAUGHT IN A TRAP

SO YOU'RE RELAXING IN THE GARDEN WITH A COCKTAIL ON A HOT SUMMER'S DAY, AND YOU HEAR BUZZING BEFORE NOTICING A FLY HAS SUBSEQUENTLY DROWN HIMSELF IN SUMMER FRUITS GIN. DO YOU POUR IT OUT AND GO REFILL, OR DO YOU USE YOUR STRAW TO FISH OUT THE JUICY FLY BEFORE SIPPING YOUR CONTAMINATED CONCOCTION? IF YOU CHOOSE THE LATTER, THEN I'M SORRY TO SAY BUT YOU'RE A FOUL FRUITCAKE.

CLONED AND CRAZY

EVER STEP INTO YOUR KITCHEN AND THINK THAT DOLLY
THE CLONED SHEEP HAS BROKEN IN AND DUPLICATED
SOME FOOD ITEMS? DON'T WORRY, THIS IS NO SCIENCE
EXPERIMENT... I WOULD WORRY ABOUT THE POTENTIAL
PSYCHO IN YOUR HOME THOUGH. YES, IT COULD BE
YOUR ROOMMATE, YOUR PARTNER, OR EVEN UNKNOWINGLY
YOURSELF... BUT OPENING MULTIPLE PACKETS OF THE
SAME THING (AND LEAVING THEM BOTH HALF FULL) IS
A SURE SIGN THAT SOMETHING'S NOT QUITE RIGHT...

I AHHHM YOUR FAHHHHTHER

IF YOU'RE SITTING IN A QUIET ROOM, AND HEAR THE
DARTH VADER IMPERSONATOR FROM THE OTHER SIDE
OF THE ROOM, THEN YOU'RE NORMAL (AND SAT IN
CLOSE PROXIMITY TO A HEAVY BREATHER). IF YOU
CAN'T HEAR ANYTHING BUT THE SOUND OF YOUR OWN
BREATHING, THEN YOU'RE THAT PERSON, AND SHOULD
HAND YOURSELF IN TO THE MENTAL INSTITUTE BEFORE
SOMEBODY GETS HURT!

A LITTLE BIT SUNNY

NORMAL PEOPLE WEAR SUNGLASSES IN THE SUN (IT'S KIND OF IN THE NAME), BUT THERE ARE A FEW CRAZIES OUT THERE WHO WEAR THEM ALL YEAR ROUND, INDOORS AND OUT... IS IT A FASHION STATEMENT? A WAY TO HIDE YOUR SOBBING EYES WHEN YOU REALISE YOU'RE NOT QUITE SANE? WHATEVER IT IS, YOU'RE NOT A LIGHT-FEARING VAMPIRE, SO TAKE OFF THE SUNNIES AND CONGRATULATE YOUR FIRST STEP TOWARDS RECOVERY!

LOGGED OUT

THIS IS THE 21ST CENTURY! COMPUTERS HAVE BECOME WAY MORE ADVANCED IN THE PAST FEW YEARS, BUT SOME PEOPLE STILL INSIST ON USING ASK JEEVES, BING, AND EVEN YAHOO INSTEAD OF SUCCUMBING TO MODERN TIMES AND USING THE ELITE SEARCH ENGINE — GOOGLE! IT'S TIME TO LET GO OF THE EARLY 2000S AND BRING YOURSELF TO REALITY. OH, AND DELETE THAT OLD MSN ACCOUNT TOO!

Psycho

🔍   bing   📷   🎤   🔍

PAVEMENT PRIVELEGE

CONGRATULATIONS! YOU'VE BROUGHT ANOTHER LITTLE PERSON INTO AN ALREADY OVER-POPULATED WORLD. THAT'S FINE – YOU DO YOU. BUT WHAT YOU'RE NOT GOING TO DO IS DRIVE THE GENERAL POPULATION OFF THE PAVEMENT WITH YOUR FOUR-BIRTH BUGGY. HERE'S A NEWSFLASH: IF YOU CAN'T NEGOTIATE A PAVEMENT WITH YOUR PUSHCHAIR, LEARN TO DRIVE... PSYCHO.

REACH FOR THE STAR SIGNS

WE ALL KNOW SOMEBODY WHO TAKES HOROSCOPES A
LITTLE TOO LITERALLY. THEY READ THEIRS DAILY,
AND INSIST ON TELLING YOU ALL ABOUT YOUR LOVE
LIFE AND HOW THE NUMBER 5 IS LUCKY FOR YOU. THEY
INVEST SO MUCH OF THEIR TIME, THAT IT'S BASICALLY
BIBLICAL TO THEM NOW.

THIS OBSESSION CAUSES FAR TOO MUCH PSYCHOTIC
ENERGY, AND SOON THEY'LL BEGIN TO RUB THEIR
FINGERS OVER THE NEAREST SNOW GLOBE IN HOPES OF
SPEAKING TO THE DEAD.

A LITTLE WOOF

SHOWING AFFECTION TO OUR PETS IS A LOVELY (AND NORMAL) THING TO DO. HOWEVER, IF YOU'RE FRENCH KISSING YOUR POOCH TO SHOW YOUR APPRECIATION OF THEIR FLUFFINESS, THEN I'M SORRY TO SAY, BUT GETTING SECTIONED IS THE LEAST OF YOUR WORRIES. DO YOU KNOW WHERE THAT DOG'S TONGUE GOES? IT LICKS ITS BUTT, ITS GENITALS, AND PROBABLY EVEN EATS OTHER DOGS POOP WHEN GOING WALKIES!

DONT BE COCKY...

YOU'RE AT YOUR LOCAL SWIMMING BATHS OR LIDO, AND
BESIDES VERUCAS, WHAT'S THE BIGGEST VIBE KILLER?
YES! MEN IN SPEEDOS. LET'S BE HONEST, WHO NEEDS
TO SEE THAT? THERE ARE CHILDREN AROUND, HAVE
SOME DECENCY! YOU'RE NOT EXACTLY COMPETING IN
THE OLYMPICS, YOU PAID £5 TO DO BREASTSTROKES IN
THE SLOW LANE FOR 15 MINUTES. DON'T BE A PSYCHO,
WEAR SOME STANDARD SWIMMING TRUNKS!

WANNA PIZZA ME?

YOU THINK YOU'VE MET THE PERSON OF YOUR DREAMS.
THEY'RE A TOTAL HOTTIE, MAKE YOU LAUGH AND COME
FROM MONEY! WHAT COULD BE BETTER? SO YOU GO
ON A DATE. THEY WANT PIZZA. YOUR FOOD ARRIVES
AND THEY BEGIN TO EAT... WITH A KNIFE AND FORK.
YES, THAT'S THE SOUND OF YOUR HEART SHATTERING.
I'M SORRY TO SAY, YOU FELL IN LOVE WITH A
PSYCHOPATH. DON'T WORRY, THERE'S SUPPORT GROUPS
FOR THIS KIND OF THING.

YOU'RE UNDER A-VEST

SO YOU BREAK OUT THE IRONING BOARD TO IRON YOUR
SOCKS AND UNDIES...
WAIT... DID YOU READ THAT CORRECTLY?

IF YOU SAW NOTHING WRONG WITH THAT STATEMENT,
THEN YOU NEED TO PUT THE IRON DOWN SLOWLY AND
STEP AWAY FROM THE BOARD. YOU'RE UNDER ARREST
FOR BEING CRIMINALLY INSANE. YOU DON'T NEED
TO SAY ANYTHING, BUT ANYTHING YOU DO SAY WILL
DEFINITELY BE USED AGAINST YOU.

DOUBLE TROUBLE

THERE'S NOTHING WORSE THAN SEEING LOVEY DOVEY
COUPLES DOING SICKINGLY CHEESY THINGS LIKE
MATCHING PHONE WALLPAPERS, KEYRINGS, OR... BRACE
YOURSELF... MATCHING OUTFITS! THESE ARE THE KIND
OF PEOPLE WHO BASK IN THE CRINGE OF THEIR PUBLIC
DISPLAYS OF AFFECTION – EVEN THEIR DOG WILL HAVE
A "BABY POOCH" OUTFIT.

IF THIS REMINDS YOU OF YOURSELF AND YOUR OTHER
HALF (YOUR CONJOINED TWIN), THEN YOU SHOULD BE
ASHAMED OF YOURSELVES! BE YOUR OWN PERSON AND
STOP LOOKING LIKE A COMEDY DUO!

PENNY FOR YOUR THOUGHTS

AFTER YOUR VISIT TO THE SHOPS, YOU NOTICE YOU'VE ACQUIRED SOME 'SPECIAL' 50P COINS. BEATRIX POTTER, BATTLE OF HASTINGS… MAYBE EVEN A KEW GARDENS COIN!

WHAT YOU DO NOW DETERMINES WHETHER OR NOT YOU SHOULD BE LOCKED UP IN THE LOONY BIN. DO YOU SAVE THEM IN A LITTLE POT IN THE HOPES THEY COULD BE WORTH SOMETHING, OR DO YOU POP THEM IN YOUR WALLET, READY FOR ANOTHER SPENDING SPREE? – IF YOU PICKED THE SECOND OPTION, THEN THE MEN IN WHITE COATS ARE LOOKING FOR YOU – AND THEY DON'T TAKE BRIBES!

FREE NUTJOB

PEOPLE SAY YOU SHOULD NEVER TRUST A SKINNY CHEF, BUT WE SAY YOU SHOULD NEVER TRUST A PERSON WHO DECLINES FREE FOOD. THAT'S RIGHT, FREE FOOD! WHEN SOMEONE OFFERS YOU A MEAL FOR FREE, DON'T TURN YOUR NOSE UP AT IT LIKE A COMPLETE NUTTER, GET IT EATEN. SO WHAT IF IT COULD GIVE YOU FOOD POISONING? IT WAS FREE, SO YOUR POCKETS HAVEN'T BEEN HARMED!

NO MAT-CH FOR ME

YOU GO TO THE PUB WITH YOUR MATES AND YOU JUST CAN'T HELP YOURSELF... RIP, RIP, RIP... YOU'VE SHREDDED UP A BEER MAT AND HAVE LEFT A PILE OF CRUMBLED UP CARDBOARD. LET'S FACE IT, YOU'RE NOT GOING TO CLEAR IT UP, AND IF YOU ARE, THEN IT'LL BE AN HALF-ARSED ATTEMPT BY THROWING IT INTO A WET GLASS. MMMM, SOGGY!

LOOK, WE'D FORGIVE YOU IF YOU SAW A HOTTIE ACROSS THE BAR AND JUST HAD TO TAKE DOWN THEIR NUMBER, BUT PEELING AND SHREDDING MATS FOR THE SAKE OF IT? THAT'S PSYCHO.

LOST THE PLOT-LINE

THE LIGHTS ARE DIMMED, SNACKS ON THE TABLE
AND YOU SETTLE DOWN FOR A MOVIE NIGHT IN. YOU
WOULDN'T WALK INTO A CINEMA SCREENING HALF WAY
THROUGH THE FILM, SO WHY, OH WHY WOULD YOU START
A FILM FROM HALF WAY AT HOME? NOT ONLY HAVE YOU
MISSED THE STORYLINE OF THE FILM, YOU'VE ALSO
LOST THE PLOT!

ATI-SHHHHHHH-OO!

SNEEZING IS SOMETHING NONE OF US CAN HELP DOING, BUT YOU CAN TELL A PERSON'S MENTAL STATE BY THE SOUND OF THEIR SNEEZES. YOU HAVE PEOPLE WHO SNEEZE NORMALLY – THESE ARE THE PEOPLE YOU CAN TRUST IN AN ASYLUM... THEN YOU HAVE QUIET SNEEZERS. COME ON, YOU'VE GOT TO AT LEAST MAKE SOME FORM OF ANNOUNCEMENT WHEN YOU SNEEZE!

WHAT ELSE ARE YOU HIDING?

ACHOOOOO!

SO YOU'RE THINKING "I MAKE A SOUND WHEN I SNEEZE, I MUST BE MENTALLY SANE!". WRONG. IF YOU SNEEZE LOUDER THAN A CAR BACKFIRING, THEN I'M SORRY TO SAY BUT YOU'RE ALSO A TARGET FOR THE MEN IN WHITE COATS. WE SAID ANNOUNCE YOUR SNEEZES, NOT SONIC BOOM THEM!

PSYCHOPATHS KNOW INTELLECTUALLY
WHAT IS IMMORAL, THEY JUST DON'T HAVE A
FEELING OF IMMORALITY ABOUT IT!

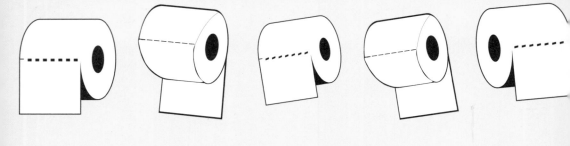

books by
BOXER

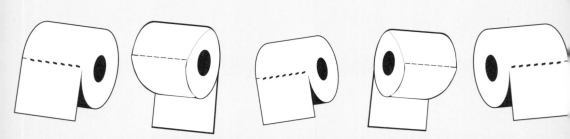